Children of the World

Czechoslovakia

For their help in the preparation of *Children of the World: Czechoslovakia*, the editors gratefully thank Employment and Immigration Canada, Ottawa, Ont.; the US Immigration and Naturalization Service, Washington, DC; the Embassy of Czechoslovakia (US), Washington, DC; the United States Department of State, Bureau of Public Affairs, Office of Public Communication, Washington, DC, for unencumbered use of material in the public domain; and Mary Anne Gross, Milwaukee.

Library of Congress Cataloging-in-Publication Data

Czechoslovakia.

   (Children of the world)
   Bibliography: p.
   Includes index.
   1. Czechoslovakia--Description and travel--1978- . Juvenile literature. 2. Czechoslovakia--Social life and customs--1986-   Juvenile literature. 3. Children--Czechoslovakia--Juvenile literature. I. Nebor, Leos. II. Knowlton, MaryLee. III. Wright, David K. IV. Series: Children of the world (Milwaukee, Wis.)
DB2022.C84 1988   943.7043   87-42638
ISBN 1-55532-241-7
ISBN 1-55532-216-6 (lib. bdg.)

North American edition first published in 1988 by

Gareth Stevens, Inc.
7317 West Green Tree Road
Milwaukee, Wisconsin 53223, USA

This work was originally published in shortened form consisting of section I only. Photographs and original text copyright © 1987 by Leos Nebor and V. Cihakova. First and originally published by Kaisei-sha Publishing Co., Ltd., Tokyo. World English rights arranged with Kaisei-sha Publishing Co., Ltd. through Japan Foreign-Rights Centre.

Copyright this format © 1988 by Gareth Stevens, Inc.
Additional material and maps copyright © 1988 by Gareth Stevens, Inc.

Typeset by Ries Graphics ltd., Milwaukee.
Design: Laurie Bishop.
Map design: Sheri Gibbs.

1   2   3   4   5   6   7   8   9   92   91   90   89   88

Children of the World

Czechoslovakia

Photography by
Leos Nebor

Edited by
MaryLee Knowlton
David L. Wright

Gareth Stevens Publishing
Milwaukee

. . . a note about *Children of the World*:

The children of the world live in fishing towns, Arctic regions, and urban centers, on islands and in mountain valleys, on sheep ranches and fruit farms. This series follows one child in each country through the pattern of his or her life. Candid photographs show the children with their families, at school, at play, and in their communities. The text describes the dreams of the children and, often through their own words, tells how they see themselves and their lives.

Each book also explores events that are unique to the country in which the child lives, including festivals, religious ceremonies, and national holidays. The *Children of the World* series does more than tell about foreign countries. It introduces the children of each country and shows readers what it is like to be a child in that country.

. . . and about *Czechoslovakia:*

Ondra Jires lives in Prague with his father, who is a movie director, and his mother, who is a computer engineer. The family also enjoys spending time at their cottage in the lovely countryside. Like his father and mother, Ondra is also creatively inclined and enjoys working with both art and computers.

To enhance this book's value in libraries and classrooms, comprehensive reference sections include up-to-date data about Czechoslovakia's geography, demographics, currency, education, culture, industry, and natural resources. *Czechoslovakia* also features a bibliography, research topics, activity projects, and discussions of such subjects as Prague, the country's history, political system, ethnic and religious composition, and language.

The living conditions and experiences of children in Czechoslovakia vary according to economic, environmental, and ethnic circumstances. The reference sections help bring to life for young readers the diversity and richness of the culture and heritage of Czechoslovakia. Of special interest is the comparative view this book offers of Czechoslovakia as a member of both the European community-at-large and the community of Eastern European nations within the Soviet orbit.

CONTENTS

The Jires family, with a movie director in its midst, knows when a camera is around.

LIVING IN CZECHOSLOVAKIA:
Ondra and His Busy Family

Ondra Jires is a 12-year-old boy from Prague, Czechoslovakia's capital city. He lives with his mother, Hana, his father, Jaromil, his 17-year-old sister, Alenka, and his mother's Aunt Eva.

North America

South America

Europe

Czechoslovakia

Asia

Africa

Australia

Czechoslovak Socialist Republic

West Germany

East Germany

Prague

Poland

U.S.S.R.

Austria

Hungary

Ondra and a friend enjoy the sunshine outside his apartment building.

Ondra's father at work.

Bicycles are used by people of all ages for transportation.

Ondra's father is a movie director. His films are known throughout the world and are very popular in Czechoslovakia. Some, such as *The Cry*, have been shown in North American theaters with subtitles or English dubbing. *Partial Eclipse* is about a little blind girl. This movie was made in 1982 and has appeared in theaters around the world.

Ondra's father has taught his son a lot about making movies. Here they study English together.

Jaromil Jires works hard. He makes about four movies a year. Besides art films for theaters, he makes documentaries and movies for television. He is especially interested in how world events affect the personal experiences of people. One movie, *My Love to the Swallows*, is about the life and death of Maruška Kudeříková, a young Czechoslovakian woman who fought against the Nazis.

Ondra's mother, Hana, is a computer engineer. She works as a systems analyst at the National Bank of Czechoslovakia. She has worked all her adult life. Her daughter plans to work, too.

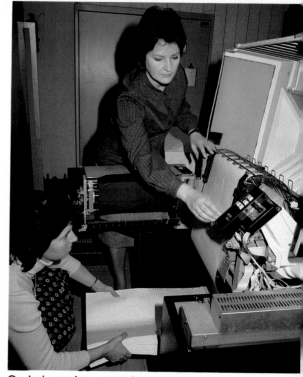

Ondra's mother at work.

Ondra and his mother try out a walkie-talkie he's made from thread.

Alenka is dressed for a dance. Ondra thinks she looks great. He's glad he's not going.

Alenka is in her last year of high school. She has a very busy school and social life. She speaks Japanese and English as well as Czechoslovakian and dances and sings in the school chorus. She loves to date and travel. Next year she will begin studying medicine at the University of Prague.

Both Alenka and Ondra speak English well. Their grandfather is fluent and they love to speak it with him. Because of their father's work, they often have house guests from other countries, and English is the language most people can understand. Sometimes their guests' English is not so good and everybody must muddle through together.

11

Sunday Dinner with the Whole Family

On Sundays Ondra's family is joined by his grandparents who also live in Prague. They have a grand meal of traditional Czech dishes. Ondra's favorite is knedlicky, a kind of dumpling made of flour, yeast, sugar, eggs, and bread cubes. It is steamed, sliced, and covered with gravy. Knedlicky is served with vepřova pečeny, which is roast pork, and a sweet and sour cabbage called zeli.

Ondra's grandfather always brings something from his garden. Since his retirement, he has made raising vegetables and fruits a fine art. Ondra's grandmother was a school teacher before she retired. Today she tutors children who need extra help at school.

Sunday meals are special, so Ondra's mother starts cooking early.

After a meal this big, an afternoon nap sounds good.

Ondra's room has bunk beds for overnight guests.

Ondra and his cardboard robot.

And Now for Ondra!

What is Ondra all about? Well, that's not easy to say in a few words. Ondra is a curious and creative boy. He loves robots, electronic games, computers, and science fiction — but not just for playing and reading. He actually built his own robot and writes his own science fiction. Once he gets started on something, he gets the whole family involved. His mother teaches him what he doesn't already know about the mechanics of a project. His father searches for materials he needs. Alenka and Aunt Eva are recruited for advice and encouragement. But the ideas are Ondra's, and he does the work. His room is full of his own inventions and creations: cardboard robots, science fiction cartoons, and electronic games.

Ondra enjoys playing with a battery operated car. Real cars are not easy to get in Czechoslovakia.

14

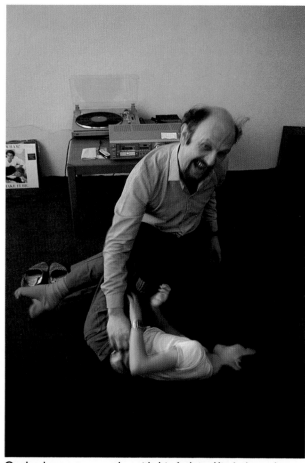

Being the youngest in a family of energetic and creative people, Ondra gets a lot of attention. They all want to show him what to do with what they know. His father and mother have passed on their love of reading and music. Aunt Eva teaches him the traditions of her native Moravia, once separate from Czechoslovakia and rich in culture. And Alenka shows him how to be cool. His favorite pastime is learning with his grandfather about how things grow. He starts the delicate plants indoors in the winter, nurtures them all spring, and watches over them until harvest time. Several years ago he planted three fruit trees which he still tends today. Next year they should bear fruit.

Ondra loves to wrestle with his father. His father always wins because he tickles.

Alenka shows Aunt Eva a sweater in a fashion magazine. She hopes Aunt Eva will knit it for her.

16

Aunt Eva keeps Ondra company while he writes a story.

At 82, Ondra's Great-Aunt Eva is an important member of the family. With both parents working, Ondra and Alenka look to Aunt Eva for help with homework and old-fashioned skills. Her help with cooking and housework during the week makes the busy household run smoothly.

Behind Ondra's apartment complex, the road narrows to a small path leading to a large field. On top of a hill in the field are the remains of an old castle. Today it isn't much more than a pile of rocks, but it's still a great place to play. Ondra and his friends create elaborate games of cowboys and Indians based on old American movies and television shows they have seen.

Ondra and a friend, Leos, explore the ruins of an old castle.

School — Learning, a Czech Child's Work

On school days, Ondra gets up at six o'clock. School doesn't start till eight, but he's slow in the morning and has things to do before he leaves. He eats breakfast and dresses and washes up. Then he packs his bag with the day's books and papers and makes a sandwich to eat with fruit for his midmorning break.

Running late.

Everything is here for a busy day at school.

...ndra checks out how a motor goes together. He'll apply what he sees to his own electronic building.

Benito Juarez Elementary School is a short bus ride from Ondra's house. It has about 1,000 students in 31 classes. Ondra is in the 6th grade. His class of 25 students is small for Czechoslovakia, where most classes have at least 35 students. Tuition, books and supplies, and lunch are free for all school children.

Children trade jokes and secrets in the minutes before the bell rings.

Ondra is good at math.

A language tape lets him hear perfectly pronounced English.

Geography is not Ondra's best subject.

Ondra takes classes in the Czech language, mathematics, Russian history, English, geography, biology, art, music, and citizenship. Math is his best subject, but English and Russian history are his favorites. He studies between five and eight subjects a day in 45 minute classes.

Ondra's class isn't crowded, though most Czech classes are.

The children line up for physical training class.

Besides his academic subjects, Ondra also takes classes in wood and metal working and physical education. The students have a break for snack at ten o'clock after their second class. Lunch is at noon. The Czechs have a large noon meal — soup, main course, dessert, and milk — which school children eat in the school dining room. Fresh vegetables and fruit are hard to get in Czechoslovakia even in season. Out of season they are unavailable, so most Czech meals are made up of heavier foods with a flour or potato base.

Raising Young Czech Citizens

Czech children participate in a wide range of after-school activities. At least once a week, children attend the Pioneer meeting of the Czech Communist Youth Organization. The Pioneers have a variety of activites members can choose from: technology, natural science, hiking, and sports like soccer and tennis. Ondra has chosen "Training and Adventure in a Natural Environment." The group leader is a high school boy who takes his group camping once a month. During the campout, they play military war games. The organization makes sure they learn and work as well as enjoy camping with their friends.

Wood and metal working class is fun for most of the children. Ondra likes working with his hands.

Students return their dirty dishes to the kitchen after lunch.

Ondra's school was designed in 1939 by Czech architect Jaroslav Gillar.

The children enjoy studying and chatting outdoors while the weather is mild.

From 4th grade on, children spend one month of each year at a Pioneer camp. Children from industrial centers and cities live for several weeks of the school term in these open-air schools in the mountains or countryside. These schools teach children the values of the Czech society and government. Here the children receive thorough guidance in how to live a happy and productive life according to the communist philosophy.

Besides social guidance training, the children also participate in athletic competitions and academic work at camp. They canoe on the rivers and in mountain streams, sleep in tents, and learn how to stay clean, warm, and dry outdoors. They also clean up the woods and collect herbs for medicines. Ondra loves camp. The outdoor experiences are fun for him and give him lots of ideas for his stories.

Czech children are taught at school — and usually at home as well — that the purpose of a good life is to work. And a child's work is to learn.

Here are some of the values Czech children hold. They hope for peace and an end to military and nuclear arms competition, although their country is a major weapons producer. They also value friendship. They share the same goals as their fellow students and expect to live and work closely with them, so friends are important. Their government tells them that working hard will bring good times for them and for their country. They believe this and guide themselves according to this hope.

After school Ondra goes home. Most Czech children are from families where both parents work outside the home. So they go to day care, called *dorgina,* after school. There they can play and study until their parents are home. But because Aunt Eva lives with Ondra, he can go home and have a snack after school. Then it's time for his chores. He is in charge of the daily grocery shopping, which he does on his bike. After shopping Ondra does his homework.

Ondra's school bus stop.

Shopping after school.

The city of Prague. The building on the left is St. Nicholas Church, famous for its baroque architecture.

The drama Theater in National Theater Complex.

Living in Prague

Everybody in the Jires family is busy during the week. They all look forward to the weekends. On Saturday mornings Ondra and his mother do their main grocery shopping. The shops are only open in the morning, so they finish their work early. The rest of the weekend is for relaxing. Often they spend part of their weekend strolling through the streets of Prague. On Sundays, the center of the city is closed to motor traffic. The streets are quiet and peaceful. People enjoy looking in the windows of the closed shops.

Sunday morning in Prague. ▶

Old streets in Prague. They say Mozart stayed here when he performed in Prague.

A doll shop.

The center of Prague is divided into three parts: the older city, the new city, and the historic area around the castle. Prague was built in the 9th century and was not severely damaged in either of the two world wars. Throughout the city you can find so many historic buildings that you feel as if you are in an architectural museum. It is truly one of central Europe's most beautiful cities.

Prague is not far from the mountains, which can be seen from the city. The Vltava River flows through the heart of the city. The many trees and park areas provide homes for squirrels and other small animals.

The buildings of Prague, old and new.

Ondra and his mother look at books in a department store.

A subway station in Prague. Public transportation is important to Czechoslovakians because 90% do not own automobiles.

A tram service runs around the heart of the city, but it's not very fast. For practical purposes most people travel by subway. Buses carry people from the subway terminals to the suburbs. Only one out of ten Czechs has a car because they are so expensive. Besides the cost, the two-year wait for delivery discourages many who might buy cars.

Some restaurants in Prague are in bright shopping areas. Others are tucked into housing projects and ancient buildings. Sometimes you have to know where a restaurant is because there is no sign outside. Small pubs serve Czech beer, local wines, and great plates of sausage, ham, and dumplings.

The government of Czechoslovakia has done much to restore Prague to its former beauty. Some of the old buildings have been cleaned and restored over the past few years. Sometimes, though, the scaffolding stays up on buildings for years with no apparent work being done. The museums, concert halls, and galleries are being well-maintained, perhaps because the government sees tourist dollars as a source of income for this hard-pressed country.

From many places in Prague you cannot see the apartment complexes that ring the old city or the industrial plants beyond them. The old city with its bridges, spires, domes, and palaces looks as it did centuries ago.

A Prague expressway.

Weekends in the Country

Often on weekends Ondra's family goes to their country cottage near the Sázava River, 40 miles (64 km) from their home in the city. The cottage was once a farm house with a large tract of land surrounding it. They have renovated the house for use as a vacation retreat.

A wood burning stove provides heat and cooks the food at the cottage. The whole family gathers wood for fuel from the nearby forests. Cooking on a wood stove or over an open fire gives a wonderful taste to the food. When the weather is good, the family eats outside. If someone has been lucky at fishing in the Sázava, there will be fish for dinner.

Wild mushrooms from the fields add a special touch to the meal.

Food tastes better outside, no doubt about it! ▶

The land that once went with the cottage is now a government-owned farm.

In the cities central heating and modern appliances are available to most people. But in the country they don't exist. So in the fall, everybody pitches in to gather firewood from the forest. They use an ax to chip it into usable pieces and stack it outside the cottage.

Chopping wood for the stove.

Picking wild mushrooms.

The wood stove cooks food and heats the cottage.

Berries on the mountain ash tree signal the end of summer.

Ondra's family has a car. Ondra loves to work on it.

Ondra checks the tomato harvest. He and his grandfather started the plants indoors last spring.

In front of the house is a corn field and a garden where Ondra's grandfather raises vegetables. In the woods behind the cottage are wild mushrooms and blackberries. Ondra's family preserves nuts, berries, and vegetables by freezing, canning, and drying them. In the winter, when the markets have few fresh fruits and vegetables, the summer's harvest will be a real treat.

Ondra's grandparents and other relatives all share in the use of the cottage. Often they are all there at once. The cottage is small, but the mood is relaxed and everyone enjoys the time together. Ondra and his cousins especially love to swim and fish in the river.

Cottages are for secret places. Nearby is a military firing range. Ondra goes there alone sometimes to collect used ammunition cases. They are his secret, and he hides them in a hole in the sloping river bank behind the cottage.

It may be the weekend, it may be the cottage, but it's still homework.

Christmas shopping on the street.

Winter Festivals — Christmas

Winter begins in November. As soon as it arrives, people start preparing for Christmas. They buy or make gifts for their families and friends. Ondra has been working for months on a science fiction cartoon story, a comic book, really, for his father. His mother, Aunt Eva, and grandmother start the holiday baking weeks before Christmas.

All the markets are busy.

40

Everybody needs a tree.

On the streets, Christmas is also everywhere. In Czech families, evergreen trees are brought into the house on Christmas Eve to be decorated from top to bottom. People bring out glass ornaments handed down from generation to generation. Children add the final touches — chocolate candies, gold and silver chains, candles, and cookies.

The open-air markets are busy with vendors selling carp, the traditional Christmas dinner dish. For Czechs, carp is a fish of good fortune. Those who eat it at Christmas will find peace, good health, and a joyful spirit in the new year.

Fresh carp for Christmas.

41

After Christmas dinner the Jires family turns off the electric lights. In the soft glow of the candles, they give each other the presents they have bought or made. While they open their gifts, they sing old songs and eat the cakes and cookies the women have baked.

More electronic games! Ondra is happy with his gifts.

The tree glistens with old family decorations.

The evening ends with midnight mass. At the church the worshippers sing songs and enjoy the Christmas atmosphere. Coming home late, Ondra his just enough energy left to look at his gifts once more. He falls asleep reading his new book.

Pouť

The most popular festival in Prague is Pouť, which means Pilgrims' Festival. Pouť is a thanksgiving festival dedicated to a patron saint. It is held in many places throughout the country. In farming communities it takes place at harvest time. People celebrate at dances and town fairs.

A firing range offers prizes to good shooters.

Ondra and his friend Leos walk through the amusement park deciding what to do.

Candy and toys are tempting.

A Czech merry-go-round.

Traditionally people made pilgrimages to churches to offer thanks for the harvest. Today the festivals are no longer religious because the government discourages religious celebrations, although it does not ban them.

In the cities that do not have harvest festivals, Pouť is usually held in winter. Matějská Pouť, dedicated to Matěj, the patron saint of Prague, comes at the end of February when the winter is nearly over. The festival lasts for a month.

The children of Prague love Matějská Pouť. They spend as many days as possible at the amusement parks. Special sweet foods and candies are part of the celebration.

Winter in Prague is a season of activity. Adults go to concerts, theater, and exhibitions. But children love the festivals and outdoor sports best.

Ondra's favorite ride is the jet coaster. ▶

Cars! Ondra loves them in any size or shape!

Skiing makes the winter fun.

Even in a large city like Prague there are plenty of places for skating and sledding. The rivers and ponds in the city freeze over into ice rinks. Ondra loves skiing behind his house in the fields where he played in the summer. Snowballs whiz across the school playgrounds and snowmen pop up in the yards of houses and apartment complexes.

It's been a good year for Ondra. He has worked and played hard. With the long winter nearly over, he looks forward to the greening of the countryside.

FOR YOUR INFORMATION:
Czechoslovakia

Official name: Czechoslovak Socialist Republic
Československá Socialistická Republika
(check-OS-lo-VEN-ska so-shall-IS-tick-ah re-PUB-leek-ah)

Capital: Prague

History

Beginnings

People who called themselves Celts and people who called themselves Slavs first lived in Czechoslovakia. No one is sure where they came from, but traces of civilization about 2,500 years old have been discovered. A bit later, tribes of German settlers moved into what is now western Czechoslovakia.

Descendants of all these people feared the Avars, who lived in what is now Hungary. But Charlemagne, the Holy Roman Emperor, defeated them in the 8th century AD. His successors brought Christianity to the country's residents. Prince Wenceslas allied his Czech kingdom with Germans and helped Christianity to

The National Theater, in Prague, at night. The Vlatava River flows in front.

spread east and north. Meanwhile, Hungarian Magyar tribes took control of Slovakia (now eastern Czechoslovakia).

The greatest of the Czech rulers was King Charles IV, who ruled from 1347-1378 during what is now called the Golden Age of Czechoslovakia. His accomplishments were many. He brought artisans from all over Europe to build many of the beautiful churches, monuments, bridges, and castles which survive today. He founded the famous Charles University, the first in central Europe. He became Holy Roman Emperor and made Prague the capital of the empire.

Religious Reform

At about the same time, 1360, the Roman Catholic Church began to come under attack for its vast wealth. Corruption in Prague, where there were many churches, was widespread. In 1402, Father Jan Hus began to preach in the Czech language instead of Latin. He told church members and religious students that the Church had strayed from its mission on earth and should return to simpler ways. He was burned at the stake in 1415, but his courage started the Protestant Reformation.

The reformation movement was carried on throughout what is now Czechoslovakia and in Germany. Feuding among countrymen continued into the 16th century and was sharpened by Martin Luther's attacks on the Church in Germany in 1517.

Followers of Hus formed the Moravian Church, which became common in Czechoslovakia. They were met head-on by a tough new group of priests called Jesuits. Jesuits attacked Protestantism with the blessing of royalty. The Jesuits and numerous noblemen persecuted Protestants. That sparked a riot in Bohemia. This and other rebellions were dealt with cruelly. People were given a choice: return to Roman Catholicism or leave the country. Gradually, most people came back to the Catholic faith. Most of the Moravian Brethren left Bohemia, first for Poland, then for Germany, and finally for the United States.

During the period from 1620 to the eve of World War I, 1914, the country was ruled by a series of Austrian kings named Hapsburg, or Habsburg. In 1860, after several years of discontent, a constitution was issued by the Hapsburg king, Francis Joseph. Yet most of the power remained out of Czechoslovakia, in the King's native city, Vienna. The years between 1860 and 1914 saw bickering between Czechs and Slovaks and between Czechs and Germans.

World Wars I and II and Beyond

Austria and Germany were eager for war in 1914, but the Czechs opposed it. Entire Czech army units crossed over to fight with the Russians against Austrian and German soldiers. After World War I, two men, Tomas Masaryk and Edvard Benes, helped create a republic composed of Czechs and Slovaks.

This angered German-speaking Czechs in western Czechoslovakia. Hitler used their anger as an excuse to take over the entire country in 1938. He did so by tricking Britain, France, and other powers. Numerous angry Czechoslovaks joined the communists, who promised to throw out the Germans.

Hitler sent Reinhard Heydrich to run Czechoslovakia in 1941. A cruel man, he was assassinated in 1942. The Germans, who had been deporting and killing Jews, killed Czech patriots in retaliation. On June 10, they killed all the men of the town of Lidice, shipped the women to concentration camps, gassed the children in mobile gas chambers, and leveled the town. Two weeks later, they did the same to another town, Lezaky. They looted and raided the country. This did not stop until the US and Soviet armies entered the country in 1945.

Tomas Masaryk's son, Jan, tried to bring democracy to Czechoslovakia. But the communists were the most popular of six political parties and they gradually absorbed or silenced the others. Jan Masaryk's body was found in a Prague street in 1948. Although it was never proven, communists probably pushed him out of a window in a government building.

The country adopted the Soviet Union's form of government and many of the tactics of Soviet leader Joseph Stalin. These included sending some politicians and religious leaders to prison or to their deaths. The persecution stopped when Stalin died in 1953, but there was little progress for individual rights.

The "Prague Spring"

In 1968, students, writers, and politicians from Slovakia forced Antonin Novotny to resign as first secretary. He was replaced by Alexander Dubček. Dubček backed several liberal reforms. Writers were allowed to write what they pleased. Students could study the subjects they wanted. People liked "socialism with a human face" so much that they begged for less government control.

On August 3, 1968, troops from the USSR, East Germany, Poland, Hungary, and Bulgaria invaded Czechoslovakia. They ordered tight control over the people and less contact with Western nations. To this day, there are Soviet troops in the country.

Since 1968, Czechoslovakia has concentrated on improving its economy. People are employed, healthy, and have adequate housing. But many writers, composers, historians, and others have been silenced by court sentences. Even though Czechoslovakia is one of the more pleasant communist countries, individual rights have never matched the high hopes of the "Prague Spring" of 1968.

Czechoslovakian writers and others continue to oppose the way all residents are treated. In 1977, they issued a request for freedom that resulted in jail for 240 people who signed the request. A request with more signatures was issued in

1978. Arrests were made in 1981, as Czechoslovakian authorities feared that a strike by Polish workers would spill into their country. Opposition to the present government continues.

Currency

The main unit of currency is the koruna, which is made up of 100 hellers.

Government

Czechoslovakia is a communist country. Communism means that all property in a country is owned equally by all the residents of that country. A German named Karl Marx first wrote about communism while living in London in the 19th century. It seemed to him to be an answer to the abuses of the Industrial Revolution that were seen in Europe at that time, where some people enjoyed great wealth while others starved in the streets and six-year-old children worked in factories. Communism in Czechoslovakia is modeled after that of the Soviet Union.

Since the Soviet invasion of 1968, Czechoslovakian officials have taken orders from Moscow and have passed on Soviet policies and regulations to the Czech people. Lately Soviet ruler Mikhail Gorbachev has initiated a policy of *glasnost*, which means "openness," in the Soviet Union. Many Czechs hope that *glasnost* will spread to Czechoslovakia and lift some of the repression there, where artists and writers operate under the strictest rules of any Eastern European country except Rumania.

Czechoslovakia is made up to two republics, one Czech, one Slovak. A federal assembly, made up of two different chambers, elects a president for a five-year term. The president appoints the premier and a cabinet. There are several major political parties, but they all are communist and work together. With trade unions and other organizations, they all form what is called the National Front. So there really is just one political party in the country.

The government's control can be felt almost everywhere. Officials make sure that history tells only what they want people to know. For example, the reforms attempted in 1968 are hardly ever mentioned. Officials say their country is in the forefront of the peace movement, yet Czechoslovakia is a leading maker and exporter of weapons. And they prevent anti-communist writers and artists from being read or seen or heard by the public.

According to Amnesty International, a worldwide organization that monitors human rights, it is a crime in Czechoslovakia to write in private letters or to speak critically of official policies, to listen to Voice of America broadcasts, and to distribute unapproved literature. An employed Czech must receive permission from the party representative at his or her place of work to visit a foreigner living in Czechoslovakia.

No one in today's Czechoslovakia is forced to join government-sponsored youth organizations. But joining these organizations is one way to get access to computer training or travel or athletic competition. That means participants have to listen to government teaching in order to do what really interests them.

Just as frustrating is the official anti-Western attitude. Any map will show that Czechoslovakia is in the heart of Europe. But the government has turned completely eastward, cutting the people off from their historical ties with Germany, France, Austria, and other countries. Czechs and Slovaks see themselves as very European. They do not identify with much of the culture of the Soviet Union. Many Czechs and Sovaks have relatives in North America who came over when leaving was easier. These people's feelings about the countries of Western Europe and Canada and the US are, therefore, less hostile than those expressed by their government. Not everybody in Czechoslovakia feels that the country is run by Czechoslovakians, and not everybody is happy about it.

Unemployment is not a problem in Czechoslovakia. In fact, labor shortages have resulted in lower production than the government would like to see. In order to increase the labor force the government provides incentives for people to have children: rent reductions, health and day care, and maternity leaves. Mothers get a subsidy for a few months after the birth of their first two children. Still the cost of housing and food is so high that the birth rate, especially in the cities, remains low.

Population and Ethnic Groups

Czechoslovakia has a population of about 15,500,000. Czechs make up 64 percent of the population. Slovaks are 30 percent of the population. Of the remaining six percent, most are Hungarians. There are also a few persons who consider themselves Germans, Poles, and Ukrainians.

The Czechs and the Slovaks have much in common and get along well. Their physical appearance is very similar, their languages can be understood by each other, and both trace their ancestry back to ancient Slavic people who settled central Europe.

The best thing a person can have in this country is a good education. Well-educated people are highly respected. Along with Communist Party officials, they may be able to obtain such scarce consumer goods as brand-name clothing, fresh fruit, or portable tape recorders. The average annual wage is about $5,100. One person in 10 owns an automobile.

Language

Czechs speak Czech. Slovaks speak Slovak. The languages are very similar and can be understood and read by almost everyone. The written languages carry many accent marks. Almost every word has some sort of slash or hook above it. Both the Czech and Slovak languages come from the same family of languages as Bulgarian, Polish, Russian, and Serbo-Croatian, which is spoken in nearby Yugoslavia.

Other languages sometimes heard in Czechoslovakia include Hungarian and German. Russian is the most popular language to study in school, with English second. Many big-city signs are in several languages, including English, German, and Russian.

The government accommodates children who speak Hungarian and Ukrainian by publishing children's magazines in these languages as well as Czech and Slovak. This assures that all children will be aware of the duties and benefits of being Czechoslovakian citizens.

Land and Climate

Czechoslovakia has cold, dry winters and hot, rainy summers. That doesn't sound very nice. But the land is often so pretty that people don't notice. July is the hottest month. Cold days occur in December, January, and February. Typical temperatures might be as cold as 0°F (-17°C) in January and as hot as 85°F (29°C) in July. Annual rainfall is as little as 18 inches (46 cm) in the center of the country to as much as 60 inches (152 cm) in some mountains.

There are some snow-capped peaks, several more than 7,500 feet (24,600 m) high. There are great, green hills that roll on for miles. And there are scenic highlands. The Bohemian Highlands are in the west and the Carpathian and Tatra Mountains are in the east.

Czechoslovakia has no seacoast, but several important rivers run through the country. The best known is the historic Danube, Europe's second longest river at 1,770 miles (2,848 km). The Danube runs east out of Austria, along the southern edge of Czechoslovakia, and into Hungary. Other large rivers include the Elbe and the Oder. Mountain streams lead to creeks and small rivers that feed the big rivers. They offer transportation, recreation, and electric power.

About the same size as the state of New York, Czechoslovakia has 49,374 sq miles (127,879 sq km). One-third of the land is covered with forests. These forests are usually spruce or beech trees. There are no trees on mountains more than 5,000 feet (16,400 m) high. Less than half of the country has soil suitable for farming.

Though it's small, Czechoslovakia borders many countries. Starting at the top of the map and traveling clockwise you find Poland, the Soviet Union, Hungary, Austria, West Germany and East Germany. Only Austria and West Germany are non-communist states.

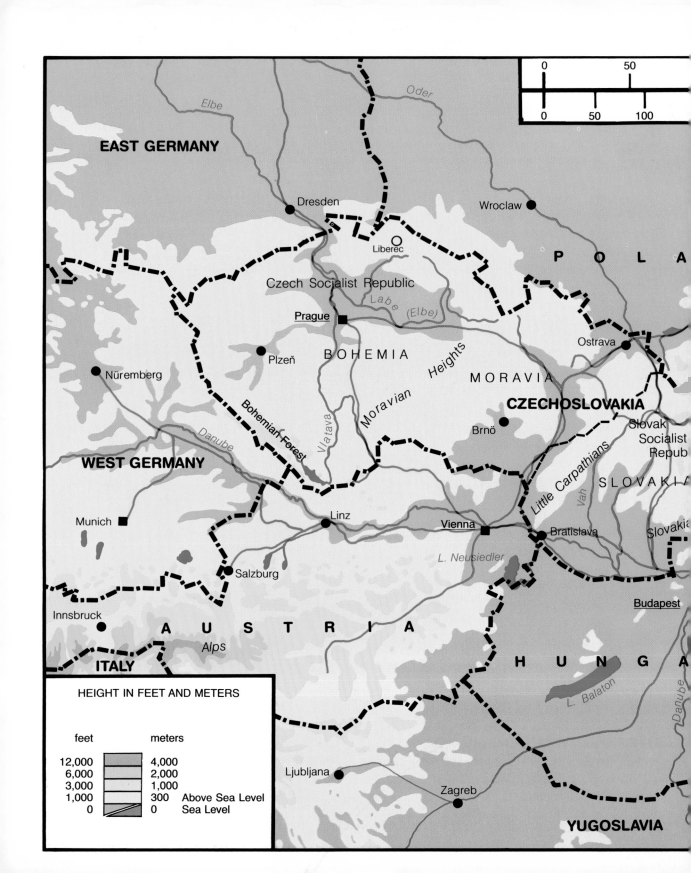

EAST GERMANY

Elbe

Oder

Dresden

Wroclaw

P O L A

Liberec

Czech Socialist Republic

Labe

(Elbe)

Prague

B O H E M I A

Heights

Ostrava

M O R A V I A

Plzeň

Nüremberg

CZECHOSLOVAKIA

Moravian

Slovak
Socialist
Repub

Brnö

Bohemian Forest

Vltava

Little Carpathians

S L O V A K I A

WEST GERMANY

Danube

Vah

Munich

Linz

Vienna

Bratislava

Slovakia

Salzburg

L. Neusiedler

Innsbruck

Budapest

A U S T R I A

Alps

ITALY

H U N G A

L. Balaton

Danube

HEIGHT IN FEET AND METERS

Ljubljana

feet   meters

Zagreb

12,000	4,000
6,000	2,000
3,000	1,000
1,000	300 Above Sea Level
0	0 Sea Level

YUGOSLAVIA

| 0 | 50 |
| 0 | 50 | 100 |

CZECHOSLOVAKIA — Political and Physical

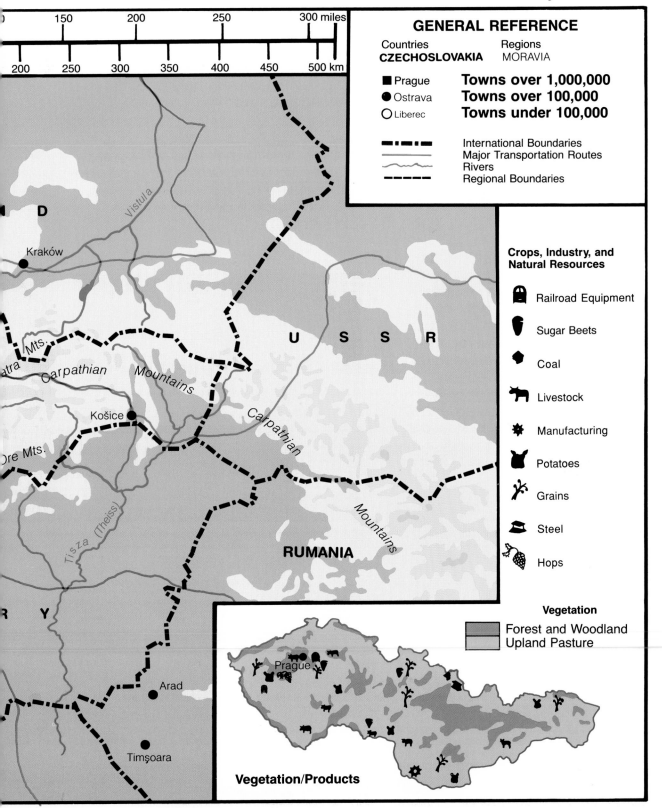

Scale				
150	200	250	300 miles	
200	250	300	350	400	450	500 km

GENERAL REFERENCE

Countries
CZECHOSLOVAKIA

Regions
MORAVIA

■ Prague — **Towns over 1,000,000**
● Ostrava — **Towns over 100,000**
○ Liberec — **Towns under 100,000**

International Boundaries
Major Transportation Routes
Rivers
Regional Boundaries

Crops, Industry, and Natural Resources

Railroad Equipment

Sugar Beets

Coal

Livestock

Manufacturing

Potatoes

Grains

Steel

Hops

Vegetation

Forest and Woodland
Upland Pasture

Vegetation/Products

Kraków

Vistula

U S S R

Carpathian Mts.

Tatra Mts.

Carpathian Mountains

Košice

Ore Mts.

Carpathian Mountains

Tisza (Theiss)

RUMANIA

Arad

Timşoara

Prague

Agriculture, Industry, and Natural Resources

Only one person in five is involved in farming in Czechoslovakia. Fifty years ago, the country was largely agricultural. But a big effort since the end of World War II has resulted in many industries and fewer farmers. Those who remain in the country are on collectives, large farms owned by the government and run according to a plan figured out by scientists and other farming experts.

Crops grown each year include wheat, barley, sugar beets, cabbage, corn, rye, oats, and potatoes. Hops are bitter flower buds used to make beer. They are grown in Czechoslovakia and exported all over the world. When the hops crop is ready, thousands of students and others are recruited to help with the harvest. Livestock is found in all parts of the country. Food growth and processing is second only to engineering as the major industry.

Engineers are trying to meet the country's demand for electricity by building nuclear power plants. Czechoslovakia is a leader among communist nations in nuclear power plant technology. However, the Chernobyl, USSR, nuclear disaster in 1986 has made Europeans skeptical of this source of power. Most of the country's energy needs are now being met with locally dug coal. Oil and natural gas are imported from the Soviet Union.

The Czech government is trying to modernize agriculture.

Electric and diesel locomotives and passenger cars are made in huge plants. They are well designed and well built. Another industry the country is involved in is arms. Many armies in far corners of the world carry automatic weapons, rifles, and ammunition made in Czechoslovakia. Other exports include machine tools, consumer goods, wood, metal-bearing ore, wood, and scrap iron and steel.

Arts, Crafts, and Architecture

Few countries can match the variety of arts, crafts, and architecture found in Czechoslovakia. Government officials have tried to preserve visual culture. They realize that many tourists are interested in the designs of the past.

Prague Castle, a huge and ancient building, is the seat of government. Preserved within its walls are a cathedral and a special ceremonial church. They are hundreds of years old. Elsewhere in Prague are examples of the great periods of European architecture: Romanesque, Gothic, Renaissance, and Baroque.

Art 1,000 years old can be found in Czechoslovakia. Paintings, tapestries, church windows, statues, carvings — they all depict Biblical stories. A walk through the National Gallery of Art in Prague shows that later Czechoslovakian artists were influenced by Western Europe.

People throughout the world who love Classical music are familiar with the work of two Czechoslovakian composers. Bedřich Smetana and Antonín Dvořák used the melodies and rhythms of folk songs in their compositions. Their music conveys a strong spirit of nationalism.

Smetana is known to the Czech people as the founder of Czech national music. His opera, *The Bartered Bride,* is often performed in the US and Canada. His suite of musical tone poems, known as *My Country* or *My Fatherland,* contains a melody called *The Moldau.* Moldau is the German name for the Vltava, the wide, peaceful river that runs through Prague from the west. Smetana's music recalls the sound of the river as it ebbs and flows through the countryside.

Dvořák is best known for his *Slavonic Dances* and the *New World Symphony.* The *Slavonic Dances* are rich and lively songs based on folk dances from Bohemia. The *New World Symphony* was composed during a trip to the United States. The lovely recurring theme is based on a Negro spiritual known here as *Going Home.*

Folk music, plus other folk arts, including glass ornaments, handmade toys and dolls, embroidery, woodcarving, and ceramics are less popular now but are still seen on special occasions and at local festivals. The lovely Bohemian glass and garnets that many immigrants to North America passed on to their children are still produced in Czechoslovakia.

Famous Czech writers known in English-speaking countries include Franz Kafka, whose work is not available there today, though it is studied throughout the non-communist world. Jaroslav Hasek's *The Good Soldier Schweik* is also regarded outside Czechoslovakia as a major 20th century novel. Poet Jaroslav Seifert won the Nobel Prize for literature in 1984.

Arts that are approved by the government, and there are many, are also supported by the government. Music and theater performances are cheap and good. A much wider range of people attend than here, where prices are often high. Musicals like *My Fair Lady* and *Fiddler on the Roof* are popular. Country Western music also has a popular following at the moment, though jazz is not approved by the government and musicians and audience alike enjoy it at some risk. Ballet, modern dance, and opera flourish. Moviemakers are among the world's best.

Besides the many art museums, Czechoslovakia has a number of history museums which contain artifacts from past periods or peoples no longer present in great numbers in Czechoslovakia, such as the Military History Museum and the Jewish museums housed in former synagogues. The history told in these museums might surprise people who know better. The Military History Museum, for example, shows only the Soviet Union fighting against the Nazis.

Religion

Communism and religion don't always get along very well. That is true in this country, where priests, ministers, and rabbis are paid by the government. Religious leaders who try to find new members or make a big public display of their religion might find their pay, home, or even freedom taken away.

Three of every four Czechs who go to church are Roman Catholic. There is a Catholic church in every city. There are some Protestants, mostly Methodist, Baptist, and Unitarian. Only older people go to church on Sunday in the big cities. However, religion is still important to many rural residents. They wear colorful folk outfits and are sometimes members of Greek Orthodox or Catholic churches.

Easter and Christmas are public holidays. But religion is not an important part of life in modern Czechoslovakia.

Education

Free education is provided to every child for 10 years, from ages 6 through 15. After that, more than half join the work force, usually in a three-year apprentice program. Those who pass a test go on to four years of high school, called gymnasium. They can also spend three or four years in a technical school or go to a farm where they join a work-study program.

At the age of 19, boys and girls who have completed a secondary school can take a test for college. There is no charge to attend any kind of high school or college. But besides passing tests, college students must pick a field of study that the government considers necessary. If, for example, there are no jobs as history teachers, then students may not study history.

In Czechoslovakia education determines social status. Doctors, professors, and lawyers are highly regarded. So are people with artistic and technical abilities. This high status, plus membership in the Communist Party, allows people to do things, buy things, and go places not permitted to others.

Sports and Recreation

Czechoslovakians take their sports very seriously. A few years ago, nationwide riots were touched off after a tough hockey game with the Soviet national team. If hockey is the most popular winter sport, indoors and out, soccer is the summertime favorite and the most popular overall.

Every kind of sport has a sponsor connected to the government. The best teams compete with teams from other countries. Next to soccer and ice hockey, track and field and downhill and cross-country skiing are very popular. So are tennis, handball, basketball, swimming, and bicycle and motorcycle racing.

Czechoslovakians have rocks and mountains to climb, streams to fish or paddle in a kayak, plus many scenic areas for camping. About one family in ten has a cabin or a hut in a rural area. City dwellers go to these cabins almost every weekend throughout the summer. They usually have big gardens on the property and enjoy hiking, picnicking, and sunbathing.

An unusual form of recreation is the spartakiad. Once every five years, children and adults from physical training classes across the country gather in stadiums to perform dancelike gymnastics. The national spartakiad stadium holds more than 200,000 spectators.

Health spas are important to Czechs, who have 37 spas with 24,000 beds. Every year 300,000 patients are treated at the spas. Spring waters are the basis of the treatment in the form of baths and drinks. Other treatments include mud and peat packs, exercise, and massage. The spas are used instead of surgery or drugs for a wide variety of diseases.

Children in a *spartakiad*, a yearly gymnastics event.

Czechoslovakians in North America

In 1848, riots and disturbances swept much of Europe. Bohemians, Czechs, Slovakians, and other central Europeans came to North America in large numbers. They settled in the US Midwest and throughout Canada.

Residents of Czechoslovakia are somewhat free to leave and return to their country with proper exit visas. These visas state where they may go. If they go somewhere not specified on the visa, they may not be allowed back in the country or may be in trouble when they return. Several hundred thousand Czechs leave each year to vacation, though they can only take a little bit of money out of the country. Then, if they don't come back, they will not have taken Czech money from the country. Czechoslovakian students who study abroad usually go to the Soviet Union or East Germany. They seldom are allowed to attend school in a democratic country.

American culture has been greatly enriched by the presence of immigrants from Czechoslovakia. They brought a rich culture and love of learning that made them successful in their new land. Willa Cather's novel *My Antonia* tells the story of a daughter of Bohemian immigrants growing up in Nebraska. Cather herself was a child of Bohemian immigrants and found great success as an American writer.

More Books About Czechoslovakia

Here are more books about Czechoslovakia. If you are interested in them, check your library or bookstore. Some may be helpful for the research projects that follow. Some are stories and folktales from Czechoslovakia.

Czechoslovak Wit and Wisdom. Martin (Penfield Press)
Czechs and the Slovaks in America. Roucek (Lerner)
Gone Is Gone. Gag (Putnam)
Land and People of Czechoslovakia. Hall (Lippincott)
My Antonia. Cather (Houghton-Mifflin)
Take a Trip to Czechoslovakia. Lye (Franklin Watts)

Glossary of Useful Czechoslovak Terms

Czechoslovakia has two official languages, Czech and Slovak. The two languages are similar — if you can understand one, you can understand the other. The following words and phrases are Czech.

ano (A-no) . . . . yes
chléb (khlehb) . . . . bread
cokolada (CHO-ko-lah-da) . . . . chocolate
dě kuji (DYE-ku-yi) . . . . thank you
dobry den (Do-bree den) . . . . hello
kostel (KO-stel) . . . . church
máslo (MAH-slo) . . . . butter
mléko (MLEH-ko) . . . . milk
ne (neh) . . . . no
oběd (OB-yed) . . . . lunch

prosím (PRO-seem) . . . . please
sbohem (SBO-hem) . . . . good-bye
snídaně (SNY-eed-an-ye) . . . . breakfast
stát (staht) . . . . stop
večeře (VE-cher-zhe) . . . . dinner

Things to Do — Research Projects

Governments and their policies can change quickly. In 1968 Czechoslovakia was developing policies that would allow people more freedom than in the past. An invasion organized by the Soviet Union resulted in restrictions that have made Czechoslovakia one of Eastern Europe's least liberal societies. Today in the USSR, the government is allowing more open expression. Will Czechoslovakia follow Moscow's lead? Or will it wait to see what happens in the USSR?

As you read about the developments in Czechoslovakia, or any country, keep in mind the importance of current facts. Some of the research projects that follow need accurate, up-to-date information from current sources. Two publications your library may have will tell you about recent newspaper and magazine articles on many topics:

The Reader's Guide to Periodical Literature
Children's Magazine Guide

For answers to questions about such topics of current interest as the Czechoslovakian response to *glasnost*, look up *Czechoslovakia* in these publications.

1. How far is Prague from where you live? Find out how you could get there, how long it would take, and what you would need to take along. Use maps, travel guides, travel agents, or any other resources you can think of.

2. Think of a career or job that interests you. Would you be able to do this kind of work in Czechoslovakia? Would being male or female make a difference? Would your ethnic background, your religion, or your political beliefs make a difference?

3. Using current magazines and newspapers from your library, see what the government of Czechoslovakia is allowing its citizens to do as glasnost takes hold in the USSR. Do the people of Czechoslovakia have things to say that are different from the government's stated positions?

More Things to Do — Activities

These projects and things to think and talk about will deepen your knowledge of Czechoslovakia. Some are group projects and some are just for you to do at school or at home.

1. As in many communist countries, the government of Czechoslovakia writes the history of the country. Some things are left out of their account. For example, the official account tells the people only that the Soviet armies freed the country from the Nazis in World War II. Actually it was a joint effort by several Western countries and the USSR. What effect do you think it has on the people of Czechoslovakia to know only part of their history?

2. Many people in Czechoslovakia and other countries where the government limits their access to information have very strange ideas about the West. Write an imaginary letter to Ondra. Tell him what you would want him to know about your life and your hopes for the future.

3. Find a tape or record of Dvořák's *New World Symphony* or his *Slavonic Dances*. Your library probably has them. Listen in a quiet, comfortable place. If you can get both works, listen to them both. Do they sound as if they were inspired by different places and peoples?

4. Invite someone from Czechoslovakia to talk to your class or a group you belong to. Here are some questions you might ask: When and why did you leave Czechoslovakia? Do you ever go back? How is Czechoslovakia different from when you lived there?

Think of other questions of your own.

5. If you would like a pen pal in Czechoslovakia, write to these people:

International Pen Friends
P.O. Box 290065
Brooklyn, New York 11229-0001

Be sure to tell them what country you want your pen pal to be from. Also, include your full name and address, and your age.

Index